THE POWER OF THOUGHT CHILDREN'S BOOK SERIES

I CAN CHECK
MY SENSES

Written by Amber Raymond & Lynn McLaughlin

Illustrated by Allysa Batin

Illustrated by Allysa Batin

ISBN: 978-1-7780741-6-5 (paperback)
ISBN: 978-1-7780741-7-2 (ebook)

Printed by Print Works
382 Devonshire Road
Windsor, Ontario N8Y 2L4

https://lynnmclaughlin.com
https://www.messsmakers.com

We all feel many emotions. The characters on the planet Tezra glow in the following colours to match how they are feeling.

Red	Orange	Blue	Yellow	Green	Purple
Anger	Scared	Sad	Surprised	Happy	Lonely
Frustration	Worried	Disappoint-ed	Unexpected Event	1 Believe in Myself	
	Uncertain				

Are You Up For A Challenge?

- Can you see when each character's feelings are changing?

- Can you tell by the look on their faces, by body language or the words they are using? Maybe you can tell by the colour of their glow.

- Have you ever felt the same way? How do you express your own feelings?

"Oh I'm so **excited** for you to teach me how to play Wabble today Carnuli," said Lazu.

"I can tell you're getting **frustrated** by the look on your face," said Carnuli. "You're glowing so red, your muscles are stiff and you're breathing heavily."

"Well, it's OK to be **angry** Lazu. I'm happy that you can feel your emotions, but let's find a good way for you to express them," smiled Carnuli patiently.

"Would you like me to teach you how to check your senses? It's something that works for me when I'm **angry**." Lazu nodded as their red glow began to dim slightly.

"When my heart is beating fast, it can be hard for me to think clearly," explained Carnuli.

"First I take some deep breaths. Pretend you're holding a cupcake with a candle in front of you.

Now breathe through your nose. Doesn't that cupcake smell great? What flavour is it? Does it smell like chocolate or vanilla?"

"Now breathe out of your mouth and imagine you are blowing out the candle. Let's do that together until you feel calm."

"Let's look around and find 5 things you can see with your eyes that make you smile."

"How are you feeling now Lazu?" asked Carnuli. "What do you think?"

"When I looked for things that made me smile it made me feel **happy** and my body started to relax."

Thankfully,

You Can Check Your Senses Too!

1. Take 3 deep breaths.

2. Ground yourself by checking your senses:

   - Find 5 things around you that you can see.
   - Find 4 things you can smell.
   - Find 3 things you can hear.
   - Find 2 things you can touch.
   - Find one thing you can taste.

3. Remind yourself that practice makes progress.

4. Try again.

Vocabulary

Angry - a feeling of being upset or annoyed by something or someone

Smell - with our nose

Taste - with our tongue

Touch - with our fingers

Hear - with our ears

See - through
our eyes

Like You, Every Crystal is Unique!

Did you notice the characters are all named after crystals?

Some crystals look like simple rocks, and others look like they're from another planet. No matter their appearance, they all make you feel a sense of wonder when you see the way they shine.

Also known as rocks, gemstones, and minerals, crystals are formed through geological processes by heat and pressure underground. Working with crystals can help you transform into the most powerful version of yourself by guiding you to see how incredible you truly are.

Carnelian (*Carnuli*): empowerment, focus, action and confidence

Opal (*Opal*): creativity, renewed hope, good karma, balance, self-regulation

Lapis Lazuli (*Lazu*): intuition, education, communication and problem solving

Sardonyx (*Nyx*): empowerment, confidence, leadership, courage, growth and boundaries

Epidote (Epido): energize, healthy, strengthen, provide hope, open you to love and joy

Amber
Raymond
BA, BSW, MSW, RSW

WWW.MESSSMAKERS.COM

As a Social Worker, Amber is an advocate for unconventional, evidence-based coping strategies and is devoted to her friends and family.

She is passionate about child mental health, lifelong self-care practices, self-exploration, self-love, and holistic wellbeing.

When not practicing social work, Amber likes to research new, effective methods to overcoming life's mental and emotional challenges.

Lynn McLaughlin

MED, BED, BA

WWW.LYNNMCLAUGHLIN.COM

Lynn McLaughlin served as a Superintendent of Education, Administrator and Teacher. Lynn now teaches future Educational Assistants at her local College.

Lynn hosts the inspirational podcast "Taking the Helm" and welcomes a new guest on Wednesdays.

As a best-selling, award-winning author and Rotarian, Lynn is dedicated to community causes. She is a member of 100 Women Who Care Windsor/Essex and works tirelessly to support the goals of the Brain Tumour Foundation of Canada

Allysa Batin

⬜ @bats.illustration

Allysa Batin is a young freelance illustrator. She enjoys creating fun and colourful characters and advocating for love and acceptance in her art. Her favourite pastimes include hosting Dungeons & Dragons and taking pictures of her dog.

She's happy to spread positivity through the book series, and hopes to continue illustrating in the future.

Other books in *The Power of Thought* Series:

I Have Choices
I Can Calm My Mind
Is What I'm Thinking True?
I Can Ground Myself